# GO FIGURE!

## More Maths Challenges for Busy Minds.

## BOOK A

### John Thompson

Published by User Friendly Resource
Enterprises Ltd. Book No. 241A

CU00646989

## TITLE

Book Name:     **Go Figure!**
               More Maths Challenges for Busy Minds.
Book Number:   241A
ISBN Number:   ISBN 1-877260-16-9
Published:     April, 2000

## AUTHOR

John Thompson

## ACKNOWLEDGEMENTS

User Friendly Resources wishes to acknowledge the work of the following people in the various stages of publishing this resource.

**Designer:**      Lisa Ferguson
                   Jumping Jellyfish Design
**Illustrator:**   Geraldine Sloane
**Editor:**        Stephen Rout and Jan Thorburn

## PUBLISHERS

User Friendly Resource Enterprises Ltd.

| *New Zealand Office* | *Australian Office* |
|---|---|
| P.O. Box 1820 | P.O. Box 278 |
| Christchurch | Annandale, NSW 2038 |
| Ph:   0800-500-393 | Ph:   1800-553-890 |
| Fax:  0800-500-399 | Fax:  1800-553-891 |

## WEBSITE

View all our resources at www.userfr.com

## COPYING NOTICE

## COPYRIGHT

**User Friendly Resources** specialises in publishing educational resources for teachers and students across a wide range of curriculum areas, at both primary and secondary levels.

If you wish to know more about our resources, or if you think your resource ideas have publishing potential, please contact us at one of the above addresses.

# Contents

# *Introduction*

This resource provides students with a further fun series of stimulating and interesting mathematical challenges intended to enrich and enhance students' other work in mathematics.

The activities emphasise problem solving and exploration. Not all the activities will appeal to all students but every attempt has been made to cater to a range of student learning styles and interests. In keeping with current trends in mathematics education there is ample scope for co-operative learning.

In using these activities with classes of my own I have encouraged group work. This stimulates discussion and mathematical argument as students develop their problem solving skills. It also provides a situation where students need to justify the accuracy of their answer to others. Group work often gives students the confidence and encouragement to embark upon tasks that they feel are too hard to do on their own.

Some of the problems are derived from 'classic' problems in mathematics. Such problems are often still unsolved and can profitably be explored in a way appropriate to the mathematical understanding of the student. These problems have an extensive literature available and can be researched by teachers who wish to examine the ideas in more detail.

## *Problem Solving*

Problem solving can be approached using Polya's model as found in *'How to Solve It'**, a foundation work in the field of mathematical problem solving. Key steps are:

- Understand the problem
- Devise a plan
- Carry out the plan
- Check and validate the answers

The final step can be a cyclical process of checking and evaluation of possible solutions. If no progress is made then the student is encouraged to revise the plan or to check that the problem has been fully understood.

* Polya, G. (1990). *How to Solve It*. Penguin. Harmondsworth. UK.

## Optimisation

A number of activities involve finding the 'best' solution. Optimisation encourages students to realise that mathematics is not just a matter of 'right' and 'wrong' answers. Problems can have various solutions, some of which are more appropriate than others. For many realistic, practical examples there are no exact solutions. The use of spreadsheets, particularly with a teacher-provided template, is a useful approach for optimisation.

## Learning Styles

The learning styles are categorised according to Greorc's model of how information is gathered and processed by learners. Information is gathered in either a concrete or abstract form and is then processed either randomly or sequentially. Thus the four learning styles referred to with each unit are as follows.

### Concrete Sequential
- Structured, practical activities.

### Abstract Random
- Interpretative and imaginative, creative and artistic.

### Abstract Sequential
- Logical, analytical, reading based.

### Concrete Random
- Problem solving, investigative and inventive.

The activities can be used in context, as different parts of the curriculum are covered in class, or could form the basis of a problem solving module in which a number of sequential lessons are dedicated to teaching problem solving skills in mathematics.

Notes are provided for the teacher with each activity giving:

- Background Information
- Level of difficulty (☆ Easy ☆☆ Average ☆☆☆ More challenging)
- Answers
- Curriculum information
- Use of appropriate educational technology
- Extension material
- Learning style(s).

# Find the Atom!

## Information

This activity involves students in using deduction and some simple geometry to locate hidden 'atoms' on a grid. Using the rules for the way the alpha particles rebound from atoms, they deduce the position of the atoms on the grid.

Playing the game as a class exercise is a good way to introduce the rules. This helps too in working out the patterns for complex collisions. (Complex collisions are collisions involving two or more atoms).

## Extension Ideas

The game can be played using more than two atoms or a larger grid. Either of these options makes the game more difficult (and possibly too hard for many students!)

### LEARNING STYLE

**Concrete Random**

- Problem solving, investigative and inventive

### LEVEL OF DIFFICULTY

### OBJECTIVES

**Communicating Mathematical Ideas**

- Devise and follow a set of instructions to carry out a mathematical activity

- Record in an organised way, and talk about the results of a mathematical exploration

**Geometry**

- Apply understanding of symmetry and reflection

## Answers

Row 5, Column 11 and Row 5, Column 13

# Find the Atom!

**SHEET ONE** • • • • • • • • • • • • • • • • • • • • • • • • • • • • • • • • • •

## Introduction

Each player needs a copy of the grid.

One player places an atom on their grid, being careful to hide the grid and the location of the atom from the other player. The other player then tries to locate the atom by 'firing' alpha particles into the grid.

After each shot the first player tells the other which square the particle would leave from. Using the results of their shots, the opponent works out where the atom is hidden.

## The alpha particles

See in these diagrams how an alpha particle rebounds when it gets near an atom.

1. If an alpha particle approaches an atom like this it rebounds straight back.

2. An alpha particle approaching like this is deflected at an angle of 45° away from the atom.

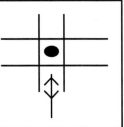

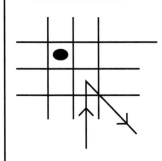

3. If an alpha particle comes near two atoms arranged like this, it moves away from the atoms at an angle of 135° to its original path.

4. If two atoms are arranged like this then the alpha particle rebounds straight back.

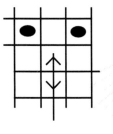

5. If two atoms are next to each other like this then the particle rebounds as shown.

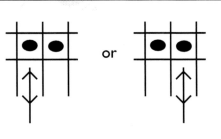

or

# Find the Atom!

## How to play

- Take turns to place an atom(s) on your grid. (Don't let your opponent see!)

- Each player starts with 10 points.

- To locate an atom, the first player says which square they are firing an alpha particle from. The second player tells them which square that particle would leave from.

- Particles cannot be fired from squares 1, 8, 15 or 22. (But they may emerge from those squares.)

- Each particle fired costs one point.

- A player's turn ends when they have worked out where the atom(s) are.

- The other player now hides atoms for their opponent to find.

- The player with the highest score wins.

### Example game with two atoms:

The atoms are hidden on the squares marked X.

| 1 | 28 | 27 | 26 | 25 | 24 | 23 | 22 |
|---|----|----|----|----|----|----|----|
| 2 |    |    |    |    |    |    | 21 |
| 3 |    |    |    |    |    |    | 20 |
| 4 |    |    |    |    | X  |    | 19 |
| 5 |    |    |    | X  |    |    | 18 |
| 6 |    |    |    |    |    |    | 17 |
| 7 |    |    |    |    |    |    | 16 |
| 8 | 9  | 10 | 11 | 12 | 13 | 14 | 15 |

| First player's move | Second player's answer |
|---------------------|------------------------|
| 2 | 21 (Nothing there) |
| 3 | 27 (Rule 2) |
| 4 | 28 (Rule 3) |
| 5 | 5 (Rule 1) |
| 6 | 9 (Rule 2) |

The first player now has enough information to work out where the atoms are hidden.

### Example game with one atom:

The atom is hidden on the square marked X.

| 1 | 28 | 27 | 26 | 25 | 24 | 23 | 22 |
|---|----|----|----|----|----|----|----|
| 2 |    |    |    |    |    |    | 21 |
| 3 |    |    |    |    |    |    | 20 |
| 4 |    |    |    |    | X  |    | 19 |
| 5 |    |    |    |    |    |    | 18 |
| 6 |    |    |    |    |    |    | 17 |
| 7 |    |    |    |    |    |    | 16 |
| 8 | 9  | 10 | 11 | 12 | 13 | 14 | 15 |

| First player's move | Second player's answer |
|---------------------|------------------------|
| 4 | 4 (Rule 1) |
| 3 | 27 (Rule 2) |

The player now has enough information to know where the atom is hidden.

The two atom game is much more interesting than the one atom game. It requires skill rather than luck.

You can play with more than two atoms, but the moves can be complicated. You may need another student to act as referee.

# Find the Atom!

**SHEET THREE** • • • • • • • • • • • • • • • • • • • • • • • • • • • • • • • • •

## *Test your knowledge:*

There are two atoms hidden.

| Fired from | Leaves from |
|------------|-------------|
| 2 | 21 |
| 3 | 20 |
| 4 | 2 |
| 5 | 5 |
| 11 | 11 |
| 12 | 12 |
| 14 | 16 |

Where are they?

**Playing grid**

| 1 | 28 | 27 | 26 | 25 | 24 | 23 | 22 |
|---|----|----|----|----|----|----|----|
| 2 | | | | | | | 21 |
| 3 | | | | | | | 20 |
| 4 | | | | | | | 19 |
| 5 | | | | | | | 18 |
| 6 | | | | | | | 17 |
| 7 | | | | | | | 16 |
| 8 | 9 | 10 | 11 | 12 | 13 | 14 | 15 |

# Guarding the Art Gallery

## TEACHER NOTES • • • • • • • • • • • • • • • • • • • • • • •

### Information

This activity derives from the 'Eight Queens' problem in which 8 Queens need to be placed on a standard chessboard so that all squares are attacked. That problem has 92 solutions. Using an art gallery as an example is a practical application for what has been a recreational puzzle. The extension activity can lead to work on tessellations as well as packing problems, if three dimensions are considered.

### Technology

• The problem can be done using scale models with light sources replacing the cameras.

• A drawing program on a computer could be used to draw the room and cameras.

**LEARNING STYLE**

**Concrete Random**

- Problem solving, investigative and inventive

---

**LEVEL OF DIFFICULTY**

☆

---

**OBJECTIVES**

**Communicating Mathematical Ideas**

• Devise and follow a set of instructions to carry out a mathematical activity

• Record in an organised way, and talk about the results of a mathematical exploration

**Geometry**

• Apply the symmetries of regular polygons

### Extension

This activity can be extended in a number of ways to make it more realistic -in particular by having the cameras cover a circular area.

For example:

Detectors are placed in the ceiling and cover a circular area of 5 metre diameter. How many are needed to protect a 20 x 20 metre room and where should they be placed?

Stated like this, the question is an example of a packing problem.

Problems of this type include:

• How much space is wasted when packing circular objects on a tray?

• What is the most efficient way of stacking oranges in a fruit stall?

Students can be encouraged to find trial-and-error solutions to such problems.

11

# Guarding the Art Gallery

## TEACHER NOTES

### Answers

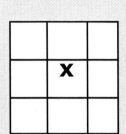
**Room 1**

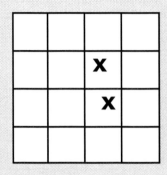
**Room 2**

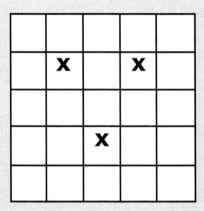
**Room 3**

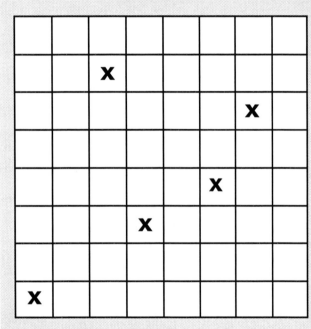

**Room 4** (5 cameras needed)

**Room 5**

**a.** 13 are necessary if the whole floor is to be covered. (Thieves often come down from the ceiling in the movies!) 9 would cover just the walls.

**b.** Circles should be drawn completely.

**c.** Four touching circles have an area of
$4 \times \pi \times 5^2 = 314.2$ m$^2$

This leaves an area of $400 - 314.2 = 85.8$ m$^2$

# Guarding the Art Gallery

## SHEET ONE••••••••••••••••••••••••••••••••••••••••••••

### Introduction

- The City Art Gallery wants to purchase special detectors to protect its rooms. The detectors work by sending out a beam in eight directions as shown in the diagram.

- Each beam can reach to the edge of the room

- The detectors are very expensive. The Art Gallery Management do not want to buy more than they need!

Your task is to work out which squares you should place the detectors on so that all the squares in each room are protected. There are four rooms for you to work on.

**Room 1:  Use one camera only.**

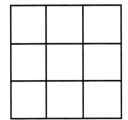

**Room 2:  Use two cameras.**

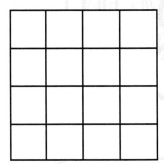

**Room 3:  Use three cameras.**

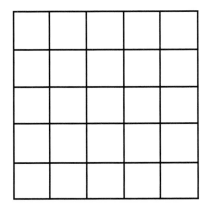

# Guarding the Art Gallery

**SHEET TWO** • • • • • • • • • • • • • • • • • • • • • • • • • • • • • • • • • •

### Room 4:

The Art Gallery has a large 8 x 8 room. What is the minimum number of cameras it needs for full coverage? Mark in where they should be placed.

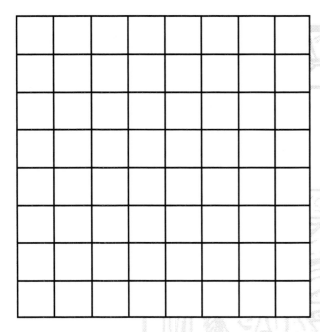

## *Now try this!*

### Room 5:

The Gallery is offered a new type of detector. These are placed in the ceiling and protect a circular area 10 metres in diameter.

You are asked to make a room 20m by 20m intruder-proof.

**a.** How many of the new detectors are needed to completely protect the room?

**b.** Draw a diagram showing where each one should be placed.

**c.** How much of the room is unprotected if only 4 of the new detectors are used?

### Hints:

It may help to use a scale diagram. You could use a computer drawing program for this.

The formula for the area of a circle is $A = \pi r^2$, where r is the radius of the circle.

# Conway's Curious Cabbages

## TEACHER NOTES •••••••••••••••••••••••••••••••

## Information

This activity is based on John Conway's Game of Life, a simulation in which cells reproduce according to simple rules. These rules, although few in number, allow complex 'life forms' to evolve.

The Game of Life created considerable interest amongst mathematicians and computer scientists when it was announced in 1970. It has connections with finite state machines and cellular automata. A very detailed account of the game and related topics is given in the reference below.

**References include:**

Poundstone, W. (1987). *The Recursive Universe*. Oxford University Press.

ISBN 0-19-285173-X

## Extension

Students can experiment with different rules for making the cabbages grow. A computer version of the game would be needed to do this systematically.

## Technology

The activity can be done using a chess board and counters of two colours - one colour for the cabbages, the other colour placed on top to indicate the cells in which cabbages remain alive (or will germinate).

Alternatively, there are many computer versions of the game available on the Internet.

A spreadsheet version of the game is available free of charge from the author. (email: euclid@ihug.co.nz)

### LEARNING STYLE

**Concrete Sequential**
- Structured, practical activities

**Concrete Random**
- Problem solving, investigative and inventive

### LEVEL OF DIFFICULTY

### OBJECTIVES

**Problem Solving**

• Devise and use problem-solving strategies to explore situations mathematically

• Use equipment appropriately when exploring mathematical ideas

**Communicating Mathematical Ideas**

• Devise and follow a set of instructions to follow a mathematical activity

**Geometry**

• Apply understanding of symmetry of a square, and others

# Conway's Curious Cabbages
## TEACHER NOTES · · · · · · · · · · · · · · · · · · · · · · · · · · · · ·

### Answers

**1a.** 3

**b. XXX** or **X** remain stable and alternate between one form and the other.
       **X**
       **X**

Note: Four cabbages are needed to create an expanding garden. Whether or not it keeps expanding depends upon the original arrangement.

**2.** –

**3a.** 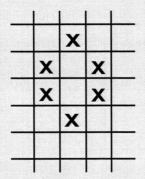 **b.**

**c.**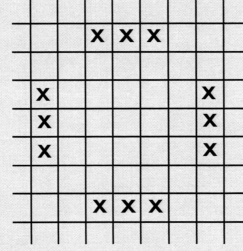

**d.** Empty

# Conway's Curious Cabbages

## SHEET ONE • • • • • • • • • • • • • • • • • • • • • • • • • • • • • •

### Introduction

The Patel family plant some cabbages in their garden. The cabbages are a new variety known as 'Conway's Curious Cabbage'. The cabbages grow in a very unique way.

1. They must be planted in a square grid - 8 x 8 is a good size.

2. If a square on the grid is empty but has 3 neighbouring cabbages a new cabbage will grow there the next day. (If it has 4 or more neighbouring cabbages, no new cabbages will grow because of overcrowding.)

3. If a square has a cabbage and has two or three neighbours, it will be alive the next day.

4. If a square has a cabbage which has less than two (or more than three) neighbours, it will die the next day!

5. All changes occur on the stroke of midnight.

The numbered cells shown on this grid are the eight neighbours of the middle cell marked with an X.

| 1 | 2 | 3 |
|---|---|---|
| 4 | X | 5 |
| 6 | 7 | 8 |

### Questions:

1. Conway Cabbage plants are very expensive. It is important to keep them alive.

   a. What is the least number you would need to plant to keep them growing?

   b. How should they be arranged to ensure that the crop doesn't die out?

To answer these questions you will need to experiment.

- Try different arrangements of small numbers of cabbages to find out which grow best. (It helps to start near the middle of the garden).

- Record the results for each day, using grids.

# Conway's Curious Cabbages

**SHEET TWO** • • • • • • • • • • • • • • • • • • • • • • • • • • •

### Example

To help you get started, here is a garden which is ready to go. Remember that the cabbages are genetically programmed to change at midnight at <u>exactly the same moment.</u> New cabbages do not immediately affect the ones that are already there.

|   | A | B | C | D | E | F | G |   |
|---|---|---|---|---|---|---|---|---|
| 1 |   |   |   |   |   |   |   |   |
| 2 |   |   |   |   |   |   |   |   |
| 3 |   |   |   |   |   |   |   |   |
| 4 |   |   | O |   |   |   |   |   |
| 5 |   |   |   | O |   |   |   |   |
| 6 |   |   | O |   |   |   |   |   |
| 7 |   |   |   |   |   |   |   |   |
| 8 |   |   |   |   |   |   |   |   |
|   | A | B | C | D | E | F | G |   |

| Cell | Number of neighbours | Condition after midnight. |
|---|---|---|
| B3 | 1 | Empty |
| C3 | 1 | Empty |
| D3 | 1 | Empty |
| B4 | 1 | Empty |
| C4* | 1 | Dies (Only one neighbour) |
| D4 | 2 | Stays empty |
| E4 | 1 | Empty |
| B5 | 2 | Stays empty |
| C5 | 3 | New cabbage (Has three neighbours) |
| D5* | 2 | Stays alive (Has two neighbours) |
| E5 | 1 | Empty |
| B6 | 1 | Empty |
| C6* | 1 | Empty (Has only one neighbour). |
| D6 | 2 | Stays empty |
| E6 | 1 | Empty |
| B7 | 1 | Empty |
| C7 | 1 | Empty |
| D7 | 1 | Empty |

\* indicates cabbage in that square.

# Conway's Curious Cabbages

**SHEET THREE**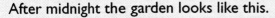

After midnight the garden looks like this.

|   | A | B | C | D | E | F | G |   |
|---|---|---|---|---|---|---|---|---|
| 1 |   |   |   |   |   |   |   |   |
| 2 |   |   |   |   |   |   |   |   |
| 3 |   |   |   |   |   |   |   |   |
| 4 |   |   |   |   |   |   |   |   |
| 5 |   |   | O | O |   |   |   |   |
| 6 |   |   |   |   |   |   |   |   |
| 7 |   |   |   |   |   |   |   |   |
| 8 |   |   |   |   |   |   |   |   |
|   | A | B | C | D | E | F | G |   |

The next night both cabbages will die because each has only one neighbour. No new ones will grow as no cell has three neighbours.

You need to be careful how you plant Dr Conway's cabbages!

**2.** Start with five cabbages. Experiment with different planting arrangements to find which arrangements will give you the most cabbages after 7 days.

**3.** Work out what these 4 gardens below will look like after 5 days. It may help to use a separate grid for each day. Start your planting near the middle of the garden.

**a.**

|   |   |   |   |   |
|---|---|---|---|---|
|   | X | X | X |   |
|   | X | X | X |   |

**b.**

|   |   |   | X |   |
|---|---|---|---|---|
|   |   | X |   | X |
|   |   | X |   | X |
|   |   |   | X |   |

**c.**

|   |   | X |   |   |   |   |   |
|---|---|---|---|---|---|---|---|
|   |   | X |   |   |   |   |   |
|   |   | X |   |   |   |   |   |
|   |   |   |   |   |   |   |   |
| X | X | X |   |   | X | X | X |
|   |   |   |   |   |   |   |   |
|   |   | X |   |   |   |   |   |
|   |   | X |   |   |   |   |   |
|   |   | X |   |   |   |   |   |

**d.**

|   |   |   | X |   |   |   |
|---|---|---|---|---|---|---|
|   |   |   | X |   |   |   |
|   | X | X | X | X | X |   |
|   |   |   | X |   |   |   |
|   |   |   | X |   |   |   |

# Television Transmission

## TEACHER NOTES••••••••••••••••••••••••••••••••••••

**LEARNING STYLE**

*Concrete Random*

- Problem solving, investigative and inventive

---

**LEVEL OF DIFFICULTY**

---

**OBJECTIVES**

**Number**

• Make sensible estimates and check the reasonableness of answers

• Solve practical problems which require finding fractions of whole number and decimal amounts

**Measurement**

• Perform measuring tasks using a range of units and scales

---

## Information

Finding the centre of an area is a problem that arises when building computer and telephone networks.

This activity involves a number of interesting geometric principles. Part A involves finding the centre of a circle which joins three points. Part B requires finding the minimum total distance from some central point to surrounding points.

**References include:**

Wells, D. (1991).
*The Penguin Dictionary of Curious and Interesting Geometry.* Penguin.

Thompson, J. (1999)
*About Geometry – Shape and Space.* User Friendly Resource Enterprises.

## Extension

**Part A** can be generalised to finding the centre of a polygon made by connecting a number of points.

**Part B** is closely linked to Steiner networks. Students could research that topic and find out how to make them.

## Answers

**PART A.** Go 20 km east and then 15 km north from Carlton. This is 25km from each town.

**PART B.** Located at 7km east and 7.5km north of Carlton. Requires 67.7 km of fibre optic cable.

**PART C.** 1. Each angle is 120°.   2. -   3. -

# Television Transmission

Go Figure!
BOOK A

ACTIVITY
4

## Introduction

Television One plans building a new transmitter for three small towns in a remote part of the country.

**Brixton is 40 km east of Carlton.**

**Acton is 30 km north of Carlton.**

Use a sheet of A4 graph or squared paper.

* Mark point C (for Carlton), near the bottom left hand corner.
* Draw a large scale diagram using
  1 km = 2 squares.
* Mark the points A, B (for Acton and Brixton respectively).
* Use the diagram for making measurements.

## PART A

Each town wants the best possible signal from the transmitter. To achieve that, the transmitter needs to be exactly the same distance from each town centre.

Find the point on your diagram that is equidistant (the same distance) from A, B and C.

It may help to record your results in a table as you try different points for the transmitter.

| Point 1 | Distance to A | Distance to B | Distance to C |
|---------|---------------|---------------|---------------|
| Point 2 |               |               |               |
|         |               |               |               |
|         |               |               |               |

How far from each town is the transmitter when all distances are equal?

## PART B

Television Three also wants to provide television programmes for the towns. They decide to use fibre optic cables to carry the signal from a transmission hub. To keep costs to a minimum, the hub is placed so that the minimum possible length of fibre optic cable is used.

* Make a new copy of your scale diagram.
* Use that diagram to find places for the transmission hub.
* Calculate the length of fibre optic cable needed for each place.

Note: The problem is a difficult one. There are many possible answers and it is hard to find the best solution. Using the Fermat method described on the next page is the easiest way to find the shortest length of fibre optic cable needed to connect the three towns.

# Television Transmission
## SHEET TWO • • • • • • • • • • • • • • • • • • • • • • • • • • • • • • • • • • •

### *One method to solve the problem: The Fermat Method.*

The problem of finding the centre of an irregular area was solved by the 17th Century amateur mathematician Pierre Fermat (pronounced fair mah). A lawyer by profession, he produced many important mathematical results. So great was his reputation as a mathematician that he became known as the 'Prince of Amateurs'.

The method he worked out was as follows.

1. Construct an equilateral triangle on each side of the triangle ABC. These triangles should point outwards.

2. For each of these triangles join the vertex that is not on the sides of ABC to the opposite vertex of the original triangle.

3. Where these lines meet is called the Fermat point. Label this point F.

4. The paths AF, BF and CF provide the shortest route linking all three villages.

### *Now try this!*

**PART C.**

1. Measure the angles AFC, BFC and AFB in your diagram. What do you notice about them?

2. Make another triangle ABC (of any size). Find the Fermat point and see if the angles are the same as in question one. Compare your answer with those of others in your class?

3. Would it be possible to find the shortest length of roads without using the Fermat method? If you can think of a possible method, try it out on an isosceles triangle with sides of 4 cm, 9 cm and 9cm.

# Up the Garden Path!

## TEACHER NOTES • • • • • • • • • • • • • • • • • • • • • • • • • • • •

## Information

This activity is an introduction to graphs, nodes and networks.

The Awataha gardens are based on Euler's Konigsberg Bridge problem. The extension activity aims at enabling students to find the necessary conditions for a Hamiltonian circuit (that is, a path which includes each node or vertex once only).

### References include:

O'Daffer, P.G. and Clemens, S.R. (1976). *Geometry: An Investigative Approach.* Addison-Wesley. ISBN 0-201-05420-5

Perl Addison, T. (1978). *Math Equals: Biographies of Women Mathematicians.* Wesley. ISBN 0-201-057093

## Extension

### ROTARY CLUB COMPETITION

The design of the gardens interests other schools. The local Rotary club arranges a competition with the following conditions.

**1.** There must be 6 gardens.

**2.** It must be possible to follow the paths and visit each garden once only.

**3.** Each garden must have more than two paths leading to it.

**4.** Each plan should have as few paths as possible.

Design a plan using the above conditions.

How many different ways are there of visiting the gardens in your plan?

## Answers

**1.** Students should be able to show they have considered all possible connnections and that none yield a valid solution.

**2.** There are a large number of solutions. Any valid combination is acceptable.

### LEARNING STYLE

***Abstract Sequential***
- Logical, analytical, reading based

***Concrete Random***
- Problem solving, investigative and inventive

### LEVEL OF DIFFICULTY

### OBJECTIVES
**Problem Solving**

- Pose questions for mathematical exploration
- Effectively plan mathematical exploration
- Devise and use problem-solving strategies to explore situations mathematically
- Use equipment appropriately when exploring mathematical ideas

**Communicating Mathematical Ideas**

- Use own language, and mathematical language and diagrams to explain mathematical ideas
- Devise and follow a set of instructions to carry out a mathematical activity
- Record in an organised way, and talk about the results of a mathematical exploration

**Develop Logic and Reasoning**

- Make conjectures in a mathematical context

# Up the Garden Path!

**SHEET ONE** •••••••••••••••••••••••••••••••••

### Introduction

The Awataha Primary school has four gardens which are joined by a series of paths as shown in the diagram.

The students at the school tried to find a way of walking along the paths so that:

• They visited each of the four gardens;

• They travelled along each path once only.

They found that it could not be done unless one of the paths was moved.

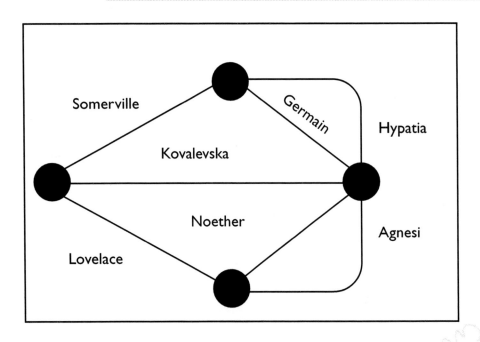

### Questions

1. Write a paragraph explaining why such a walk is impossible. Your answer should use mathematical language.

2. Redraw the diagram with the path changed so that the conditions are achieved.

3. Each of the paths is named after a famous woman mathematician. For each of them see if you can find out

   a. When they lived

   b. What type of mathematics they were famous for.

# ANCIENT MATHEMATICS

## TEACHER NOTES • • • • • • • • • • • • • • • • • • • • • • • • • •

### *Information*

The activity looks at how numbers were represented in different number systems in the past.

The work provides an opportunity for reviewing place value and the role of zero.

A study of the history of numbers would be a worthwhile research project for students.

**References include:**

McLeish, J. (1991). *The Story of Numbers.* Ballantine Books. ISBN 0-449-90938-7

Guedji, D. (1996). *Numbers: The Universal Language.* Thames and Hudson. ISBN 0-500-30080-1

Gheverghese, Joseph, G. *The Crest of the Peacock - Non-European Roots of Mathematics.* I.B. Tauris and Co. ISBN 1-85043-285-6

### *Extension*

Students can research some other number systems, and find out how to use them. Suitable choices include:

  Hindu

  Chinese

  Arabic

  African

## ROMAN

Roman numerals are still used on clock and watch faces. Years are sometimes written using Roman numerals.

1.  a.   XXIII
    b.   CCLVI
    c.   CLXVII

2.  a.   XL
    b.   CM
    c.   XXIX

3.

| Number | Roman form |
|--------|-----------|
| 456 | CDLVI |
| 226 | CCXXVI |
| 1999 | MCMXCIX |
| 1066 | MLXVI |
| 457 | CDLVII |
| 1840 | MDCCCXL |
| 99 | XCIX |
| 1974 | MCMLXXIV |
| 3600 | MMMDC |

**LEARNING STYLE**

**Abstract Sequential**

- Logical, analytical, reading based

**LEVEL OF DIFFICULTY**

**OBJECTIVES**

**Developing logic and reasoning**

• Classify objects, numbers and ideas

• Use words and symbols to describe and continue patterns

**Number**

• Explain the meaning of digits in a whole number

# ANCIENT MATHEMATICS
## TEACHER NOTES• • • • • • • • • • • • • • • • • • • • • • • • • • • • • • • •

### Answers

**MAYAN**

1. a. ●●●●    b.     c. ═══    d.

2. a. $24 = (1 \times 20) + 4$     b. $66 = (3 \times 20) + 6$

   c. $210 = (10 \times 20) + 10$    d. $391 = (19 \times 20) + 11$

3. a. $512 = (1 \times 400) + (5 \times 20) + 11$

   b. $2001 = (5 \times 400) + 1$

**AZTEC**

a. $23 = (1 \times 20) + 3$

b. $9345 = (1 \times 8000)$
$+ (3 \times 400) + (7 \times 20) + (5 \times 1)$

# ANCIENT MATHEMATICS

## Introduction

In the past, different cultures have used a variety of number systems. It is from those systems that our own number system developed.

This activity is about those systems and how they were used.

## Roman numerals

The ancient Romans used these symbols:

| Symbol | Number |
|--------|--------|
| I | 1 |
| V | 5 |
| X | 10 |
| L | 50 |
| C | 100 |
| D | 500 |
| M | 1000 |

These symbols are still used today.

Make a list of places where you have seen Roman numerals used.

**Here are the rules for using Roman numerals.**

1. Numbers are written from left to right.

   For example 37 is written as XXXVII (That is 3 tens, 1 five and 2 ones).

2. No symbol is used more than three times in succession.

3. If I, X or C are placed to the left of a higher numeral then their value is <u>subtracted</u> from the numeral on the right.

   For example:

   9 is not written as VIIII but as IX (That is 1 less than 10).

   400 is not written as CCCC but as CD (That is 100 less than 500).

Use the rules to answer these questions.

1. Write these numbers using Roman numerals

   **a.** 23       **b.** 256       **c.** 167

2. Write these numbers using Roman numerals

   **a.** 40       **b.** 900       **c.** 29

**3.** Complete this table using the rules for Roman numerals

| Number | Roman form |
|--------|------------|
| 456 | |
| | CCXXVI |
| 1999 | |
| 1066 | |
| | CDLVII |
| 1840 | |
| 99 | |
| | MCMLXXIV |
| 3600 | |

# ANCIENT MATHEMATICS

## SHEET TWO • • • • • • • • • • • • • • • • • • • • • • • • • • • • •

## Mayan numerals

Mayan numerals are made using only two symbols. They are:

●          ▬▬▬

The dot (or stone) stands for 1

The line (or stick) stands for 5

Numbers from 1 to 19 were made using the stone and stick symbols.

For example 12 is written as that is 2 ones and 2 fives.

These symbols were used by the Mayan priests for calendar calculations.

1. Write these numbers using Mayan numerals:

    **a.** 4       **b.** 6       **c.** 10       **d.** 19

To write numbers larger than 19, a base 20 system was used.
Their numbers were written vertically and read from top to bottom.

These examples will help you understand the method.

Number

43      =    2 x 20 + 3 x 1

The Mayans would write this as:

2 ●●

3 ●●●

A space is left between each level.

Number

113     =    5 x 20 + 13.

The Mayans would write this as:

5
▬▬▬▬

13

# ANCIENT MATHEMATICS

**SHEET THREE** • • • • • • • • • • • • • • • • • • • • • • • • • • • • • • • • • • •

**2.** Write these numbers using Mayan numerals.

    **a.** 24    **b.** 66    **c.** 210    **d.** 391

### A challenge:

To write numbers between 400 and 7999 another level was needed.

**Example :**

  623  =  (1 x 400) + (10 x 20) + (3 x 1)

Using Mayan numerals this becomes.

1  ●

10  **═══**

3  ●●●

**3.** Write these numbers using Mayan numerals:

**a.** 512           **b.** 2001

### Aztec numerals

The Aztec number system used just four symbols.

| Symbol | Value |
|--------|-------|
| Stone  | 1     |
| Stick  | 20    |
| Insect | 400   |
| Person | 8000  |

Numbers were written by combining these symbols.

Numbers were written from left to right with the highest value symbols on the left.

**Example :**

500 = (1 x 400) + (5 x 20)

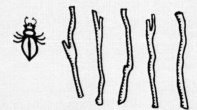

500 =

Write these numbers using Aztec symbols.

    **a.** 23    **b.** 9345

Go Figure!
BOOK A

ACTIVITY
7

# All Black Training Camp

## TEACHER NOTES • • • • • • • • • • • • • • • • • • • • • • • • •

**LEARNING STYLE**

*Concrete Random*

- Problem solving, investigative and inventive

**LEVEL OF DIFFICULTY**

☆ ☆ ☆

**OBJECTIVES**

**Communicating Mathematical Ideas**

- Use their own language, and mathematical language and diagrams to explain mathematical ideas

- Devise and follow a set of instructions to carry out a mathematical activity

- Record in an organised way, and talk about the results of a mathematical exploration

**Number**

- Make sensible estimates and check the reasonableness of answers

- Solve practical problems which require finding fractions of whole number and decimal mounts

## Information

The problems in this activity can be investigated and solved by trial-and-error methods. It is essential that students record their solutions as they proceed.

The activities involve optimisation. They are intended as accessible examples of NP (non-polynomial) problems. NP problems are problems in which the number of possible solutions increases exponentially as new data is added. They may require a heuristic rather than an algorithmic approach.

In the Tug-of-War and the Rafting problems it will help if students write out the player's name and weights on individual cards.

**Reference:**

The bootlace problem is mentioned in *The Magical Maze* by Ian Stewart (1997), Phoenix.
ISBN 0 75380 514 6

*Technology*

Calculator

Spreadsheet

## Answers

The NP nature of these problems means that a number of correct answers are possible in some cases. The solutions below are not necessarily the optimal answer.

**1 a.**

| Todd Blackadder | 105 |
|---|---|
| Mark Carter | 100 |

and

| Alama Ieremia | 98 |
|---|---|
| Blair Larsen | 107 |

**b.**

| Todd Blackadder | 105 | Charles Riechelman | 105 |
|---|---|---|---|
| Mark Carter | 100 | Robin Brooke | 112 |
| Alama Ieremia | 98 | Michael Jones | 98 |
| Jonah Lomu | 118 | Blair Larsen | 107 |

**c.** To do this effectively students will need to use a method that matches players of equal weight and then allocate the rest in the same way they did in a and b.

**2.** –

**3.** 10m from A. Total distance = 134.6m

**4.** American 77.4m  (Shoe store 86.8m  European 86.0m.)

# All Black Training Camp

## Introduction

The 1998 All Black Training squad had a number of challenges during their training.

## 1. Tug O' War

In this activity, the All Blacks had to find teams for a tug of war competition. To make things fair the total weight for each side had to be as equal as possible.

The team numbers did not have to be the same for each team.

**a.** The players available for the competition were:

| Player | Weight (kg) |
| --- | --- |
| Todd Blackadder | 105 |
| Mark Carter | 100 |
| Alama Ieremia | 98 |
| Blair Larsen | 107 |

Work out who should be in each team.

**b.** A number of other players were watching the competition. The following players decided to join in:

| Player | Weight (kg.) |
| --- | --- |
| Robin Brooke | 112 |
| Michael Jones | 98 |
| Jonah Lomu | 118 |
| Charles Riechelman | 105 |

How could these players be included so that you still had two teams of nearly equal weight?

In answering this question you are not only finding an answer, but trying to work out an effective method for choosing players so that the weights for each team are as even as possible.

**c.** Once you have worked out what you think is a good method, try it out for a tug of war involving all the players.

| Player | Weight (kg.) |
| --- | --- |
| Robin Brooke | 112 |
| Michael Jones | 98 |
| Jonah Lomu | 118 |
| Charles Riechelman | 105 |
| Carlos Spencer | 90 |
| Tana Umaga | 100 |
| Olo Brown | 110 |
| Christian Cullen | 84 |
| Josh Kronfeld | 102 |
| Scott McLeod | 100 |
| Anton Oliver | 110 |
| Mark Robinson | 86 |
| Glenn Taylor | 108 |
| Joeli Vidiri | 90 |
| Todd Blackadder | 105 |
| Mark Carter | 100 |
| Alama Ieremia | 98 |
| Blair Larsen | 107 |
| Justin Marshall | 88 |
| Caleb Ralph | 84 |
| Ofisa Tonu'u | 94 |
| Jeff Wilson | 91 |
| Tane Randall | 101 |
| Andrew Mehrtens | 84 |
| Mark Mayerhofler | 95 |
| Walter Little | 90 |
| Ian Jones | 104 |
| Norm Hewitt | 110 |
| Craig Dowd | 118 |
| Adrian Cashmore | 90 |
| Andrew Blowers | 105 |
| Carl Hoeft | 114 |

# All Black Training Camp

### SHEET TWO ● ● ● ● ● ● ● ● ● ● ● ● ● ● ● ● ● ● ● ● ● ● ● ● ● ● ● ● ●

## 2. Rafting

The All Blacks decide to go white water rafting. The rafts can hold any number of people, but their total weight is not to exceed 500kg.

Your challenge is to work out a method of allocating All Blacks to rafts so that you use as few rafts as possible.

## 3. The Sprint

During their fitness session players faced the following challenge.

The players lined up at point X. They then had to run to the goal line and then up to point Y.

The line XA is 25 metres long.

The line AB is 50 metres long.

The line BY is 100 metres long.

Where along the line AB should a player run to if they want to get from X to Y via the goal line by the shortest possible path?

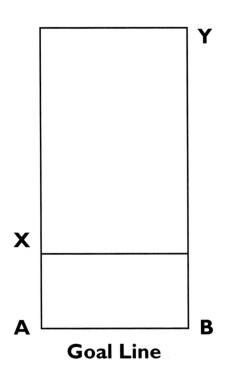

**Goal Line**

**Hint:**

There are a number of ways of solving this problem.

It will help to use a scale diagram.

With that diagram you can use:

- Measurement
  or

- Mirror lines and similar triangles
  or

- Formulas (Pythagoras).

# All Black Training Camp

## SHEET THREE ●●●●●●●●●●●●●●●●●●●●●●●●●●●●●●

## Now try this!

**4.** Another training activity was called Bootlaces. In this the players had to choose one of three different paths to run between 8 pairs of poles set out as shown in the diagrams below. You can see from the diagrams how the activity got its name from three different ways of lacing up a rugby boot.

Your challenge is to work out which path a player should choose if they want the run to be the shortest of the three possibilities.

The horizontal distance between the circles is 5 metres and the vertical distance is 2 metres. These diagrams are not to scale, so you will need to make your own diagrams.

### a)   American

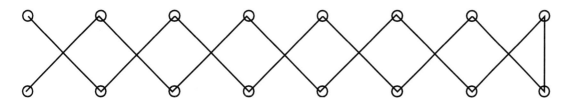

### b)   Shoe store

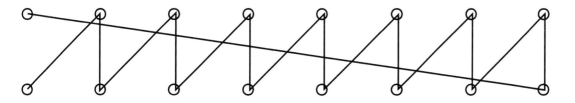

### c)   European.

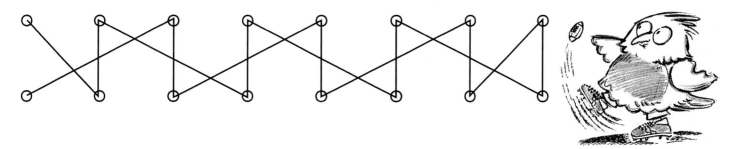

# The Secret Codes of Ari

## TEACHER NOTES

**LEARNING STYLE**

*Abstract Sequential*

- Logical, analytical, reading based

*Concrete Random*

- Problem solving, investigative and inventive

**LEVEL OF DIFFICULTY**

☆☆

**OBJECTIVES**

**Problem Solving:**

- Effectively plan mathematical exploration
- Devise and use problem-solving strategies to explore situations mathematically
- Use equipment appropriately when exploring mathematical ideas

**Developing logic and reasoning**

- Classify objects
- Classify objects, numbers and ideas
- Interpret information and results in context
- Use words and symbols to describe and continue patterns

## Information

The codes used in this activity are based on a variety of methods, often involving some kind of transposition of letters. Students can be encouraged to research or develop other methods of encoding messages.

**References include:**

*The Number Book* by John Thompson (1996) published by User Friendly Resources, contains activities based on ciphers.

## Extension

Invite the students to investigate the use of trapdoor codes, such as the RSA code. The method is difficult but can be done by very able students.

## Answers

**1st message**
I THINK THAT THIS ONE IS TOO EASY TO FOOL ANYONE

**2nd message**
THE QUICK BROWN FOX JUMPS OVER THE LAZY DOG

**3rd message**
THIS MESSAGE IS NOT TOO HARD IF YOU ARE CLEVER ENOUGH

**4th message**
WILL ANYONE EVER WORK THIS OUT

# The Secret Codes of Ari

**SHEET ONE** • • • • • • • • • • • • • • • • • • • • • • • • • • • • • • • •

## Introduction

When Ari was given a detention after school, he spent his time working out how to send messages in code.

Before the detention was over the supervising teacher confiscated Ari's coded messages but was unable to decipher the messages.

Can <u>you</u> work them out?

**1ˢᵗ message**

**ENOYNA LOOF OT YSAE OOT SI ENO SIHT TAHT KNIHT I.**

**2ⁿᵈ message**

**TH  QCK  BRWN  FX  JMPS  VR  TH  LZY  DG**

**3ʳᵈ message**

**XLMW  TLZZHNL  KU  QRW  WRR LEVH KH  BRX
DUH IRKBKX KTUAMN**

With this message Ari also left part of his method. The note read:

> Use the length of the word to work out where to start your Caesar code.
>
> For example THE has three letters so start the Caesar code with :
>
> A = C, B = D, C = E etc.
>
> For example.
>
> THE becomes WKH (shift along three letters).

**4ᵗʰ message**
**I  WNN  YLAELO  OKOT  IETV  RSWH  EUR**

The note Ari left with this said:

> I started with 1 A, 3 E's, 1 H, 2 I's , 1 K, 2 L's , 2 N's , 3 O's  2 R's, 1 S, 2 T's , 1 U, 1 V, 2 W's and a Y from a Scrabble set and then I swapped them all around except for U, I think this one will be hard to break.
>
> Hint:  The E's and O's were swapped with each other. Similarly A and Y, and so on.

• • • • • • • • • • • • • • • • • • • • • • • • • • • • • • • • • • • • • • • •

35